For anyone who feels alone.
And for Amy,
Jesse Heid,
Cherie Healey
& Him.

Cover photo
by Eraj Asadi

I LOVE BEING A WOMAN
assorted thoughts & poems

by Sarah Durham Wilson

These thoughts and poems were birthed from an ego- or identity- death I experienced after a lifeless winter in California. I had moved to the west coast from Martha's Vineyard for what I thought was love, but it was another break of the heart, which served to open me further and further. The death of the old identity began, as deaths do, a new life - of self and world discovery.

With my home of the island as my destination, I was driving my sweet old geriatric jeep, Sally, back across country. I had driven one third the way when I entered the Land of Enchantment, New Mexico. And it was there, after that dark stagnant winter, where I felt my soul's light re-spark, and I began to write again -- this time, not essays, but poetry.

I first spent a week at Ghost Ranch, where Georgia O'Keeffe once began her love affair with that wild, red, purple and golden land. They say this is the land between heaven and earth, where the veil is the thinnest. And I felt her there, I heard her there, and also heard the beginnings of my own new, truer self.

This new me was less inclined to please, more driven to be free. I was lying on the floor by the heater on a chilly March morning when I first heard her, clear as my own thoughts, and I began to write her words down. I've heard I'm not the first woman, feeling stuck and alone, to be moved by Georgia's strong, autonomous voice in those rooms at Ghost Ranch.

I then spent two months in La Puebla, before landing in the land of Taos, where I rented a beautiful casita called *House of Little Woman Magic* and felt at home, cradled in the Santo de Cristo mountains in the heart of the historic district, by a beautiful park called Sunset. On the edge of that park I'd greet a caramel colored therapy horse, who'd press his large velvet nose flat against mine, as if to teach me not to fear the big things, or even, life itself. Taos changed my life for the better. Taos helped me see who I was. Taos freed me from the prison of my small self, who worried so much what others thought, it crippled me. I offer you these words from here, this magic world of Taos.

GEORGIA & NEW MEXICO & GHOST RANCH.

All I know is I gotta get back
to New Mexico
All I know is I'm on way
Back to Santa Fe.

Ghost Ranch

We strolled along the cliffs of the canyon
and Georgia said,
My dear
Don't you dare
look at your phone
here .

GR

I can't seem to leave here
It feels like I'd be leaving
Me.

GR

A mystic poet stopped by my room
right before I went to bed
and told me something Rumi said,
That *Rushing*
drops the key
to the door
you were looking for
(And it's you
you're the door
I've been searching for.).

And Georgia said,
A woman must seek the love of herself
Before
The love of a man.

And Georgia said,
Walk Away if he makes you Part
with your Art.

And Georgia said,
You mustn't let men
Distract you from your pen.
 And Georgia said, *Hey, you:*
Don't just dream. Do.

GR
March 7th.
The day I stopped trying
Because it Never
Ever
Worked.

GR
I have to stay here
I am writing up a storm
here
I am finally
being Transformed
here.

GR
How does it happen that one comes so alive
in a place called
Ghost. Ranch.

GR
Where I just read and write and ride everyday
Because nothing else seems
to be taking this heartbreak away

GR
Out in the canyon I hear
Messages to share
Healing words to offer
Into the world's hungry air

New Beauty

Looking out at the canyon
I found a new definition of beauty
I look up to the strength and the stillness of
the rocks.
About my worth and looks-
I'm no longer on the fence
Here I stand in
Self-Possession and Confidence.
(This desert strips
Your illusions away
The desert is where
Your true self
Comes out to play.)

New Me. Xico.

This is how
I thought it would go
I thought I would come
to New Mexico
Take a break from boys
Ride a horse and buy some turquoise
I didn't know I'd dance with my shadow in the desert
and I'd be forced to look at
all the needs I hadn't met yet
I didn't know the real deal.
That I'd get so sick I'd finally heal.

She Really Let Herself Go.
Oh,
New Mexico, that land that shatters ego,
Where she really let
herself go.
Out here in the canyon
she's not looking for a male companion
She'd grown tired of looking outside of herself
for her self
and instead found her art
and tended to her heart
like a garden which now flourishes
in a place she never even knew she wanted to go,
in a quiet corner of New Mexico,
where you leave the digital noise
and the sky turns turquoise
where the wind rages and the coyotes cry and the wild
wins.
Maybe that's what it takes --
the final heartbreak…
after break… after break…
To see that you don't have to look
for what you already are;
That would be like a star
looking for light
Like the moon looking for night
Like an eye looking for its socket
When the key is always
right in your pocket.
But what will people say?
Perhaps that she really
Really, really
let
herself
go.
She says, I dare you
to go to that place
that scares you.
She says, that's where I found me
She says, that's where I got free.

LOVE

He's Like Drinking.
I can't think about him
Because it always makes me want to
Drink about him, and he,
He's like drinking
Afterwards I can never remember what the fuck I was thinking
He's fun, just at first
Then it gets messy
Then it hurts.
Why do I pick you up
Every two months
So you can let me fall
Why do I reach for you
at all
Just to be reminded
that you hurt
Just to be shoved
back down in the dirt.
And it always takes too many days
to rise back from my grave.

You Wanted to Be a Star.
You had somebody who wanted to love you
Just as you are
But you, you wanted to be a fucking star.
And now look, look how alone you are.
It doesn't matter if the whole world loves you
You've only won
when you're deeply seen
by the one.

Way Back When.
There was this time
when everything in my life just seemed to fall in place
like a rhyme
the birds sang directly to me
and when I walked, the winds graced the chimes
and everything happened right on time
it was back back back way back
when you were mine.

Let Him Choose You.
Let him choose you
When he chooses you
You don't have to do anything
But be you.

Queenhood I.
If you can't treat you
like a Queen
He can't treat you like a Queen.

You-ion.
Everything is seeking and eventually
comes back into union.
You were meant for you-ion.
There are two of everything of you:
two hands, two feet, two eyes, two breasts
two knees
two thighs, two eyes,
Two…
You know what I mean
Two sides of a heart
Long ago torn apart
So that naturally
Means
There are two
of *You*
and you are bound
to find your other you.

Fairy. God, Mother.
I said, *I lost him.*
And I want him.
Now, what do I do?
She said, *My darling, my darling*
the only thing you can ever do
is You.

Love Chooses You.
I thought he was perfect
I thought he was the most beautiful thing
I had ever seen
I said, *Yes, Yes, thank you, God*
He will do.
But you don't choose love
No, Love
chooses you.

A Terrible Thing.
It's a terrible thing to do
To love someone who doesn't love you
It's a terrible way to live, you see
To long for a love that will never be.

If It Was Meant to Be.
Oh darling, don't you see
If it was meant to be
It would be.

Titanic.

It's like you're swimming along in life
And you hit the iceberg of
A certain age
Struck, you realize, fuck,
you really are going to die
You can see it in the lines around your eyes
Your story really will end
And you might die alone
And not even have your own home
And then you have a panic attack, and
like a drowning woman
You reach for anything -
ok-
anyone- to save you
And nothing,
ok- no one does
So you finally surrender
And let go
And then are carried
Right to Him.

He

When I finally discovered
There was someone out there
Who mirrored the hidden parts of me
I rarely let anyone see
It was then, in the reflection of He
All my fears
dissolved into the sea
I was free
to finally be me
Because if I could love him
I could love me.

True Love, True You.

To find your true love
You've got to find your true you.

Love Can Come Looking for Me
I had a dream where I stood in the center of the sea
And straight in to me I could see
That all my life, the tides
had always gone out from the middle of me
But that night
They finally swirled back toward me
And that's when I knew
I'd stopped looking for Love.
That's when I knew
Love can come
looking for me.

You Can Let it Go
This is true love:
You can let it go
And it stays
Anyway.

Dark Magic
You can't talk
Or guilt
Or pray
Or spell
Or potion
Someone into loving you
You don't get
to control
Another soul.
I know you're feeling tragic
but spiritual manipulation
is the dark kind of magic.

Queenhood II.

When a prince is offering you crumbs of love
and a King is offering you a Feast
You pull up a chair next to the
King's seat.
(A Queen only ever Feasts
Can you imagine
A Queen
settling
for crumbs?
No- that's
just
dumb).

Mystic Man

They told me to cool it
They told me to water myself down
if I ever wanted to be found.
But I didn't, I stayed on fire
and I found a mystic man
he wears a king's crown
& quenches my desires.

I Was Found

I was finally found
by a love so true and tender
The most beautiful things happen
When you surrender

Narcissist

Only a narcissist wants a lover
Who's just like me
I want a lover
As mysterious and endless
and deep
as the sea

You're My Dream
Oh, the humanness,
and oh, the epicness of you
You're the dream
I pray comes true.
My favorite sound
is yours, and my favorite shape
is you
and you're the dream
that finally came true.

My Hymn to Him
Since I've met him
I have never felt
so seen
and I've never again had to ask
do you know what I mean.
Since I met him
I'm at home
In my own skin.
Since I met him
I don't feel I have to change
for him
I feel like, I can stay
strange
for him.

Ego Cage

I was lying right beside him
But I couldn't touch him
and he couldn't touch me
I was in my ego cage
I couldn't get out
And he couldn't get in
And the little girl within
Sobbed a sound that broke
The heart of the angels
and it was then
I knew I had to change
I had to leave the cage
My ego wrote a suicide note
And it died so I could live.
It died so I could love
and be loved
and not just from above.
I fell from hubris to humility
and gained humanity
to restore my sanity.

Walk Tall

true love doesn't make you feel small
true love makes you bigger
true love makes you walk tall.

Baby Bird

She said, *Forcing it breaks it*
She said, *Haven't you heard*
You have to hold love
like a tiny baby bird.

Red Flag Fire

All those red flags
Blazed into a bonfire
I knew I should have listened
To my self that is higher

Eternal Heart.

You know those flowers that are crushed by concrete
Yet after their destruction
they still rise though the cracks
in a holy eruption
That's your heart.

Soft & Holy.

Who am I?
I'm a
A soft and holy mystery
So -- *kiss me*

Not a Cool Fool.

I asked *How come every time I see him*
I feel like such a fool
And She said *Because you're so cool*
Until the minute
You try *to be cool.*

He is the Key.

He held the key that
unlocked every door
I don't think I even felt alive before-
In fact I'm sure
I was dead
before he said
My name.

Can't Fuck Fantasy

Fantasy's fun
But eventually I found it rather boring
It can't fuck you
in the cold and lonely morning.
And Rumi is nice
but his touch
is cold as ice.
From books & quotes I can no longer feed
Your aching beating heart
is all the spirituality I need.

For You
I would stand in front of a thousand trains for you
I would go to the driest desert
And make it rain
For you
I would walk across the sea
Climb the world's tallest tree
You hold the key
To my heart's every door
It is your soul
I want to forever explore.

Rock Journalist
I was a rock journalist
Then a poet of the rocks in this grand canyon
Where I realized something about me
I needed my man to be
as steady as a rock,
Because I'm the feminine
I change with the weather
I need a man
Who can keep it all together.

Him & Me & the Sea
I'm striking a balance between loving him
and loving me
so that we come together
like where the land
kisses the sea.

Into Me See
I used to close myself off and smoke too much
Now I much prefer
intimacy's naked
and trembling touch.

MY SO-CALLED LOVE

I can't wait
To get over you
God, I'm going to feel brand fucking new
It's going to feel so good
to feel good again
I'm going to find myself a car hood
and I'm going to get up and dance
and I'm going to take off my pants
I'm going to take off my bra
and everyone around me will stand in awe
at my naked courageous vulnerability
and they, in turn, will all be set free
I can't wait till I really let you go
My soul will feel like the first day of spring
After an endless winter of snow
And all those times I reached for you what I couldn't see
Was I didn't need you
I needed me
I'm gonna feel so free
I'm gonna meet all those other beautiful fishies in the deep blue sea
I'm gonna remember what it's like to have fun
I'll dance in my bedroom to *Blister in the Sun*
Just like Angela Chase
that first day she didn't wake
thinking of Jordan Catalano's face.

De-Wall Me

Please hold me in your arms all day
And take the isolation of my ego away.

You're a Seed Being Watered
Think of a seed buried in the dark moist womb of the earth
in the rain
And think of all the growth from the tears and the pain
Think of the seed buried in the wet earth
And all the beautiful ways it
It will bloom in its rebirth
Maybe it's true
that the Goddess has her own timing
Maybe it's true
that nature and the seasons
just might be wiser
than you.

WAKING WOMAN

Allow the Now
We were talking about perfection
When I said, *We're never going to get there*
so we might as well
be here.
And she said *I know that, but*
How and
I said *All we can do is*
Allow the Now.

(*Now is where the wow*
is
Now is where the pow
er is.)

She's the Drill

She feels like everyone else is standing there
Just chatting away on the surface
And she is always the drill pushing down into the dark
heart
of things.
Mining for the gold
for the truth
that has yet to be told.
But she's learned, not everyone
Wants their hearts touched
For some people
it's far too much.

It's Up to You

The thing is,
At the end of your life,
You can't blame anyone else
for what you did
or didn't do
Because it was
Always
Up to you
And every time I've taken someone else's advice
I have dearly paid the price.
There is not a deeper pain around
Than that of the woman
Who ignored her own inner sound.

Miss Mystery

What does it mean
to *let it be*
it means allowing
the mystery
Tell me why, my friend
You always demand
to know the end.

Out of the Sheets & onto the Streets
What am I going to do
crawl back in bed and watch Beetlejuice for the ten millionth time
or am going to go outside
write my books
declare my truth
and make a life
I can proudly call mine.

Guacky
We had this dog
we thought she was dumb
because she just loved
and accepted
everything
and everyone
and now I think, no, now I know --
she was the smartest
being
I'll ever know.

Ashes to Ashes
One day I'll just be dust
so live,
live I must.
Our days are numbered
and I wish I could take back
Every one
through which I slumbered.
All those years
I wasted in my head.
All those years I wasted
in my bed.

In·tune·ition
"I Told You So."
 Love,
Your Intuition

(Follow that I've got a feeling
feeling.)

Lessons. I.
You inevitably pay
for the easy
way.

Lessons II.
There will always be more to do
But there won't always be more time to be.

Lesson III.
I don't want to have to learn that lesson again
Next time it will not
Show up as a friend.

Lesson IV.
Choose potency
Over popularity.

Taken in the Storm.
It was taken from you
in the storm
So that when it came back
In whatever form
You would no longer take
it for granted.

Don't Steer in Fear.
It's all so clear
The worst decisions I ever made
I mean the ones that hurt me
the ones that hurt others
Were made out of fear.

Hey You,
Stop talking it.
Start walking it.

Leaving it Behind
She said she was so tired
And I said, you must be,
with all those bags
you've been carrying around.
Why don't you simply
Put them down.
And in that release she breathed
Like a leaf
When it falls
From the tree
like something that didn't even know
how badly it had been dying
to be free.

Bold Gold
You can play it
small and safe
or
you can play it
Big and Out There.
(Bold is where
the Gold
is, and something I've often been told,
is that most of us quit
right before
we strike gold.)

Mountain Musings

I want to stand on the mountain top and shout
"Hurry, hurry
time is running
out."

MOM

I wear my late mother's perfume
So her scent still fills the room

Wounds' Words

Pain reveals
What is asking to
Be healed.

Chance to Change

Always take the chance
to change
If you're smart
You will let life
Break your heart.

No Rise without a Fall

If you did everything right.
That would be an endless day.
There would never
Be the dark of night.

And the dark is where we mine for gold
the dark is where we release the old
the dark is where we transform
the dark is where we are born
again.

So without the dark
You would never learn
Anything at all.
Remember - there is no rise
Without a fall.

Wallflower
You enter life's dance
By taking a chance.
(She listened to her intuition, and so she took a chance—
And man, man alive-
How we watched
Her dance).

Trapped in the Tower
The ivory tower in the fairy tales is the ego
the princess can't get out
and no one can get in.
But wait, it's not fin --
She gets kissed by her inner masculine
Awakes
Takes
Action
Breaks
the wall, and answers her true call.

Last Moments
Sometimes I have to think
Do I want to die
Doing this
If this were my last moment
Would I want to be taking a selfie
scrolling Facebook
or thinking terrible thoughts about me.

Life's Sea
On that day
Life greeted me with such urgency
Dive, she said,
Dive into Me
and then I said,
Yes
to losing myself
to something so much vaster
than me.

Stalling Makes us Sick.
We get sick when we know
What we have to do
But don't do It
There's only one way out-
And it's in to it.

Before the Buzzer
What do you want to do
Before you die
and if you haven't,
Why?

How to Grow; Don't Know.
The only thing I know
Is that you never
Ever know
and allowing that is how you grow.
and the other thing I've begun to see
is that the World is always waiting
For You to Be Happy
Because when you are in your joy
You are exactly
Where you are
Supposed to be.

Oh
I had a plan but-
there's no stopping
God.

And
I forgive
because it's just
the easier way
to live.

And Once Again
if you died today
what would make you super bummed
that you hadn't done.

Dream Deaths
Giving up on your dream
Is no light thing
It takes a huge fucking toll
For it's giving up
On your very soul.

Answer Me
She said, *You can cure it*
I'm sure of it
But first here's a question you need to answer
in all sincerity
Do you believe you can heal?
Do you believe you can get free?
Take a moment to think on it
And don't just speak to please me.

Wholeness
The feminine dreams
the masculine does
So are you balanced
Are you whole
Are you standing up
and speaking out
For your soul?

This Moment
We are always so trained on the Next Moment
meanwhile This Moment is like, *"Fuck you*
what does she have
that I don't
I gave you all of me,
meanwhile she
is no guarantee."

Me
I don't need to be fixed
I don't want
to be saved
I'm taking a road
That's never been paved.

The Stuff You Don't Want to Hear Will Liberate You
It's nobody else's fault
That you're not having
the time of your life
Because this is your only time
And this is your very life.

GOD/DESS.
(Spirit, Love Consciousness, Higher Self)

Wholy Cup
Open Up
Let the Divine Fill You
Like a (w)holy cup
with which
to serve
the self so you can serve
the other
like the holy Mother.

Strong Song
Dear Women
I heard Goddess sing a song
she'd been trying to get us to hear
for way too long
She sang,
stop apologizing
for being strong.

And Then She Said
There is nothing you can do
to make me stop loving you.

That Not Alone Feeling
I have this crazy feeling
about something I can't see
I have this soothing feeling
that God is always with me.

And I Also Believe
If Spirit asked you to do it
Spirit will walk you through it

Listen-in
Listen to the inner voice
Said the angels
You just have to trust-
And know
That that voice is us.

Micro Prayer
Dear God,
Please grant me the grace
to see every face
through the eyes of Love.

I Am You
When I lose my connection to myself
I lose my connection to you
Because you are me
and I am you.

Reminder
Worrying
is doubting God.

("I can't believe I worried about that."- You, Tomorrow.)

Mirror, Mirror
I can see straight through
Your heart
All the way to God.

Empty Mystery
God says, *"If you hand me that dying thing,*
I'll hand you something new and true."
(but can you be empty-handed for a moment
can you fill your hands with faith
in the empty space).

Teaching Prayer
Dear Spirit
Teach me how to teach them
Teach me how to reach them
With Your Love.

Crystal Clarity
Once in a while
In my clarity
I can see
what God is doing
Every once in a while I get a glimpse
Of what She's got brewing.

Lean In
Darling, I'm not saying you're bad
I'm not saying you've sinned
But you're always looking for a way out
When you should be looking
For a way in.

Oops

If God lives within me
Then I better be really, really good to me.

That Place Where God Breathes

Don't listen to your thoughts
Listen to your breath

I say *I don't want to hear me*
I want to hear God
I want to go to that
place where God breathes.

The Silent Voice

Close Your Eyes
Can You Hear It?
What?
Spirit.

Healing the Other Heals Me

I feel like shit, I told the Mother
And she asked,
Well, when was the last time you did something for another?

Lakshmi

"Ill tell you what I've told you before
that it's a bore
to be poor
and you don't have to live
that way anymore."

What If

What if God/dess said,
You can stay here
If you love yourself
What if she said *I'll let you live*
If you dance for me
What if she said
I'll let you live
If you laugh for me
If you are happy for me
What if she said
I'll let you live
If you trust me
What if she said
I'll let you live
If you chase your dream for me
If this was your last chance
Would you dance?

Water Toast

Every time I don't drink
God raises a cool class of water
In a toast
To his beloved daughter.

Drowned in Love

The Goddess unleashed a tsunami of love on the planet and we all
drowned
in it and we were all
found in it.
You've been warned:
And you can't take cover, lover:
Love is coming.
And none.
Will be spared.

Spirit Songs

If there's one message from Spirit that's stayed with me
It's to let it be
and be
ye
Not
afraid,
for I am with thee.
And
I need your trust for me
To be as deep
And wide
As the sea.

Lilith

I was Lilith, exiled from Eden

They cast me out, and they never let me back in

They cast me out for not being pretty, polite, and thin

For my nakedness and desires, they told me, I was living in sin.

I was the first wild woman, I was the first witch

they left me dying in the ditch

they hunted me for dead

they said,
"Follow the rules, or we'll have your head"

I was cast out because I couldn't behave

But now I'm rising from my grave

Now I'm leaving the dark cave

Now I'm the epitome of what you call brave

Because the feminine,

We've got a world to save.

Inanna

I'm still hung up
On that last man in my bed
the one who left me
for dead
Hung up
Like Inanna on the meat hook in the underworld
Draining her blood
to die and rise whole
to lose everything but
her soul
Only the fearless know what I mean
When you finally die to the princess
and rise to the Queen.

Durga Doll

I wish when I was little
I wasn't given a Barbie with which to play
With her tiny waist and huge boobs
pink convertible and skinny legs
and a blond hunk named Ken.

I wish they'd given me Goddess Durga
with a crown in her gown
Like a lion
On her throne
And powerful
On her own.

Kali Speaks

You call yourself a wild woman?

Kali cried, *That's a lie!*
In the face of fear you always shrink
And you care so much
About what people think
On that page of yours you seek to please
But truth doesn't coddle
Truth brings you to your knees
You say what you think
They want you to say
You haven't the courage to walk the other way
Even if no one follows
So you carry on doing
What makes you feel hollow
There won't be any world left to save
If you keep walking the way
That's already
Been paved
I am in a rage
At you
For putting your wild soul back in a cage
And you've let yourself fall back asleep
Now you're lying in a hole six feet deep
You haven't one second left to please
I am screaming from the bottom of your soul
Do you hear me?
Stare me in the face
Hear the cries of the dying world
Pick back up your sword
Be authentic with your word
Stare at me until your soul
Shakes back
Awake
Radical girl of mine
Align your spine
With the throne
And grow a golden
Backbone.

Phoenix Evolution.

Out of the broom closet and into the fire
They tried to kill me but I only rose higher

You Have to Start the Car.
Meditation is like this
You have to get in the car
and sit
and you have to start the car
but then Spirit
Will drive it.

Kali II.
She said, *I'm sorry to wake you*
Just kidding
I meant to.

She's the Other
The men are crying *"You MUST PLEASE me!!"*
They're using so many exclamation points in their fear and frustration of the ground cracking
beneath their feet, as the Goddess rises from the underworld, that I go blind with helpless
rage and retire to bed.
And the women are coming from their heads
and not their hearts
tearing each other apart,
Hissing, *"I'm more Goddess than you. No, I am! No, I am!"* as if they could own, as if we could
own, the Force which owns us.
As if one woman could have more God in her than another,
for She is the Other.
So I retire again into my dark night,
I surrender without a fight,
I unclench from my ego and fall back
into the black
water.
I don't *manifest* for me, for more,
I pray for this world at death's door,
I pray that we will turn our lens away
from our own bellies and ego's desires
and turn it once more, to this world on fire.

Creativity: You have to strike
When you've been struck
and the things you're afraid to say
you have to say
anyway
and if it no longer feels like yours
you have to be willing
to close those doors.

SHE

She said, *anyone can find the miracle in the spiritual*
your work is to find the miraculous in the mundane
Once you can do that
Your life won't ever be the same.

She said,
Here's the deal
Only love can make you real

She read in a book at lunch
To never ignore a hunch
Unless you want
to feel the punch.

She said,
I'll give you some advice, very informal.
Your problem is
you're trying too hard to be normal.

She asked me, *"How did you learn
to be the way you are"*

I said, "My d*arling
know this to be true…
for you, too.
That
no one taught me
how to be me.
Instead they'll try to teach you
to be anything but you.
I had to fight so hard to get free
I had to fight so hard to be me.
But I had to be myself
I had to take that dive
it was the only way
to survive."*

She said,
*Here
is something I want you to hear
The Brave
Do what they fear.*

"Do you trust me?"
I asked
She asked me *"Do you trust yourself?
Because only if you trust yourself
Can I trust you,
too. "*

Every time I shake and look down and back
She asks
Do you trust the path?
And the way I answer her
is by walking
further.

Be In This Place

She said, *here is where*
I want you to be
In the place
Where no matter how beautiful his face
you can lose him
But not lose you.

She said, *always make sure*
You know
that at any given time-
You could go.

She's quick to admit
What she doesn't know
She sees sickness as an invitation to heal
And challenge
As a chance to grow.

She says in a voice so clear, it sings
If you want to stop feeling the same
Pain
You have to stop doing the same
things.

She woke up in the middle of the night
with something that felt
like the opposite of fright
Something that told her
Everything
Was going to be alright.
(I want to be the one
to tuck you in at night
and tell you that everything
is going to be alright).

The secret, she said,
if you know what I mean,
is to heed the whisper
before it becomes a scream.

She called me across the canyon that day
she said *come closer, never run away*
the way to get
from there to here
Is to look forward
To what you fear.

She was starting to leave when she stopped at the door
then She said,
Can you do me a favor
And I said, *Sure,*
She said, *Let's all just love each other*
that much more
She said, *you have to open your heart*
until it feels
like you're being torn apart.

She said,
Your heart
Is braver
Than your head.
Trust your heart, and forget
that thing
that fear said.

She has such a strong sense of faith
Or maybe it's surrendered vulnerability
She seems to see things
Others can't see
"Spirit," she says,
"Walks with me."

"Go ahead,"
She said,
her eyes shimmering in a dare.
"Put yourself out there
If it meant healing your self and the world,
Would you finally be ready to share?"
She said,
"The World Needs Your Medicine, Woman.

WAKING WILD WOMAN.

Self Love I.

Self love isn't just about loving your self when you're doing awesome and everything's going amazing.

It's super easy to think I'm rad when I'm killing it.

But I don't need self love when it's easy

I need it when it's hard.

I need self love when I drank wine,

even though I've been taught ten million times

with soul & body scars to prove it

That it doesn't work for me.

I need self love when I betray myself by not listening to

or sticking up for myself

When I eat til it hurts to fill the hollow

When I go to the Instagram

of the man

who rejected me and I did not need a psychic, to tell me that would hurt,

and oh yeah look, there he is with a new girl, and she's thinner and younger than me.

And her one outfit costs more than my whole wardrobe and damn she looks good in white cashmere but who doesn't?

White cashmere will treat you like the Queen that you are.

I need self love when

I pander to those who don't love me

Like, panhandle busk *So You Think You Can Dance* audition for it

Instead of falling back into the arms of those who don't make me earn it.

I need self love in the aftermath of when I thought once again

Someone outside of me could save me or I could leapfrog onto their path, and abandon this endlessly dark patch of mine

I need self love when I bulldozed all the red flags

Until they became a bonfire

I need self love when my house is a mess and my life reflects it

When I'm late on bills and promises

And I'm licking my wounds in a ditch

When people are mad at me or think I'm crazy or a passive aggressive bitch

That's when I need self love

I need it when nothing fits

Not my clothes or my old skins or the new ones- yet

When I discover more wrinkles and at the same time, more zits

I need self love

When I go to weddings alone
and smile that haunted, dead behind the eyes stare
And on Friday nights I'm always home in my lair
Because I'm too tender for Tinder
and I'm waiting for the one
even as the clock ticks
and they tell me, I'm under the gun
I need self love
When I walk into these old pits
I've fallen into again and again
And all my friends say "You knew that lesson,"
But I did it anyway
Maybe just to see if this time I wouldn't die
this time I'd fly.
I need self love.
When I feel like I'm failing Life School
Not when I'm getting gold stars
When everything gets so dark and hazy
That's when
I need to love myself like crazy.

Find Your Feminine
*Look around
at the world on fire.
Clearly it's our turn,
we wish we hadn't had to wait,
Until everything got so dire.
It's not that we don't love men
We just need everyone now,
To find their feminine.*
Love, the Women.

Nun Nor Saint

Sometimes I am in my surrender and my stillness, and sometimes
I want to put on my finest gown
and go break every heart in town
then run so far I can't be found
I may be a spiritual woman
But I have way more fun
than a nun
and here's something I ain't:
a saint.

Why, Women?

I don't understand
all this female jealousy and competition
If we all rise into the light
Does anyone's face feel less of the sun?

We're Baaaaaack

Witches are back
With the force
Of a thousand horses
Because the planet has had
All it can take
And this time
You can't tie us
To a stake

Don't Give Up

I don't ever really give up
I may stop, slow down, change direction
But I don't give up.

One of Those Days

It was one of those days where I felt stronger than wood
it was one of those days where someone asked me
why I didn't do what she had told me
and I said I was allergic to the word *should*
It was one of those days where I felt lithe and strong and ready for a fight
It was one of those days where I felt darker and silkier and sexier than night.

I Feel Real

God, she screamed, *Do you always have to say what you feel?*
Do you always have to be so fucking real?

Wild Horses

whenever someone tells me what to do
that doesn't ring true
the wild horse inside of me
rears on her hind legs and rebels
like hell.
I'm a wild fucking horse.
Me playing small for you
Will only lead to divorce.
If you really think I'm listening
when you tell me what to do
You've got another thing
Coming to you.

Self Love II.

How much love can you show yourself today?
Go ahead
Blow yourself away.

Validation

The validation will only ever be enough
when it comes from you
not when it comes from them
and not when it comes from him
no, no, no, it has to be
from within.

Stay

Find the tenderest part of you
And stay there.

It's True

The angels are begging you
To love you.

Never Turn Your Back

She said ,
"Not everything is as it would seem
Never turn your back
On a girl with a dream."

First Question

She said *"My first question in the morning*
needs to be,
how kind can I be to me?"

You Know That Part

He touched the back of my heart

you know the dark and scary part

he said,
What if you could melt your own heart
With kindness?

Am I Home Yet?

Every mistake

I make

Is me just fumbling around in the dark

in my innocence,

blindly touching the face of danger, asking

every stranger,
"Is this love?"
"Am I home yet?"

What's Your Problem?

Your problem is you've forgotten how miraculous you are

Your problem is you've forgotten

You've traveled so incredibly far

Your problem is you've forgotten all the good you've done

And that just by being you,

You've already won.

That Voice
You know how sometimes
You hear that voice from above
calling *Darling*
Can you love yourself
Enough
to be Loved?

Thank You
Thank you for the opportunity to Practice Love
every day
in every way
with every creature
with every abandoned part of yourself
with every unloved feature
and bowing to every obstacle
as a teacher.

Not An Option.
It's actually not an option
To love yourself
To not
is a death sentence.
You will get sick
and you will die
and there will never be a question
As to why.
She wasn't happy
They will say
While wishing they could have taken
your pain away.
(the world is waiting
for you to be happy.)

Self-love. III.
The world stops to pause in awe
when you learn to love your flaws.

Face of Your Heart II.
Can you look at the Face of Your Heart?
Can you listen to the tales she wants to tell you
who she's lost
how she's fought
what makes her tick
what makes her sick
what she longs for and
what makes her what to die
Who and what she wants and why
how you ignored her cries
how she's hurt
how she's healed.
Can you look
right into
the face of your heart.
Can you take her in your hands
And kiss her thirsty lips.
Don't make her suffer any more
Yours is the love
She's been waiting for.

I Am Love
I am love in the face of a fear-storm
I never die
just take a new form.

Witchy Woman
Do you hate her because she's so untamable
Because she makes you feel something
so unnamable.

Wild Woman
I don't speak the same language
as you do
I speak the one of the earth
the ancients
and the creatures, too.

Art

Scooping your heart out,
serving it to the starving world,
and gathering one's courage in the dark
to sing,
isn't the easiest thing,
but it's
the only thing.

Bad Witch vs. Good Witch

"Fuck," said the bad witch
to the good witch
"Knowing you
you'll only rise again
Knowing you
you'll be supported by all your friends
ones you didn't even try to make
ones who can't help but love you
because you're anything but fake.

Fuck," she said with a frown
"you really can't keep
a good witch down."

Stop the Slaughter.

She said, *It's in my nature*
to protect nature.
To stand
against the Slaughter
of our Mother
and Daughters.

Masc/Femme
When we *Man-ipulate*
we're in our masculine.
When we surrender
We're in our feminine.
All this need for control
cages the soul
The feminine constantly surrenders to life like a lover.
She lets it take her
She lets it shake her
She lets it wake her.

Caging our Wild (Nature.)
Why is it in our nature
to want to cage
That which is free
and kill or make mild
That which runs wild
and stifle the cries
of our inner child
and disbelieve what we can't see
and demand to control
the mystery.

Releasing Control & Saving my Soul
I looked at the little girl dying within
And knew if I wanted to save her
I had to be bigger
I had to be bolder
I had to be braver
I knew it was up to me
to give my little girl
the world.

Smart Hearts
Kindness isn't weakness
It's brilliance
the kind have discovered
the other is the self.

spring 2015
That was the spring I took my life into my arms
I vowed to age with pride and grace
I vowed to love
the lines upon my face.

My insides are growing stronger and more beautiful
as my outsides wither and sigh.
My breasts and thighs
are starting to die
they droop and drop and fall away
And I have less to giggle about
and more to say.

Womb of the World
Your vagina
smells like fish
Because the womb of the world-
life's ocean -
lives inside of you
And at every moment
You can die
and rise born anew.

Queenhood III.
Be like a Queen
Sitting in her Throne
Watching her Thoughts.
Like her subjects
She can cast out
or call in
whatever she wants.

Birthing the New Earth
She walks around with a revolution
Baking in her belly.
Its birth
will bring the new earth.

Bleeding Hearts
Things that bleed and never die
must be the most powerful, right,
says I
So, I bleed from my womb,
and I bleed from my heart
I realize these must be
my most powerful parts.

Time to Fly.
Eventually there is no self-help course left to
try
No astrology to scry,
There is nothing left to buy
You just have to step out of your cage
And fly.

Presence is Peace
The Ego loves its stories
But the soul is just presence,
living peacefully
in present
tense.

Rebel Hearts
To the Rebel-Hearted Ones, I salute you.
To those who cannot help but Love
When they're supposed to be cool
Who don't bow to the rules
I salute you.
(To Make a Difference, We Must Be Different).

Liberation
Within the choice to not react
But to respond
and if so
how
and when
lives total liberation
lies nothing short
of the miracle
of self-creation.

Royal Walk
Walk so high
with your head in the sky
Keep your spine straight
like you're walking
through Heaven's gate.

Surrender
After years of hurting and being hurt
I finally just lay down in the dirt
And the fighter died into the lover
and I let myself grow
into someone I truly wanted to love
and to know
Sometimes lying on the floor
and saying you can't take a step more
is the first step to becoming
the woman you adore.

Growing Wings
How do you fly?
You take a risk and close your eyes.

Leaving it Behind
I lost my story in the fire
Now I'm just one with life
and all my feverish desire.
Without my old story
I can rise
into my true destiny
of glory.

Don't Rush The/A Goddess
I tapped my foot impatiently and the Goddess
hissed *Never rush me*
and then She explained,
if I didn't want to feel her wrath further
I myself, should never rush either.

No Pedestal Please.
Don't look up at me
I will only let you down
Look in me
like a mirror
And please don't
Fear Her
-
(Everyday it's getting clearer
You're only just ever
Looking in the mirror)

Morning Mantra:
I've decided today
is going to be easy.
It isn't silly and it isn't sappy
To get up every morning
and choose
to be happy.

Snake Skin
I'm melting
I'm molting
this form of me is dying
I'm angry, I'm crying
I release all the parts of me
That were lying.

Break the Mold
We live in a culture
Where the weird
Are Feared
But Be Brave
Defy Convention
Become
Your own Invention.

Patriarchy's Playground.
Patriarchy made me feel
like I had to be little
To be loved
Like I had to play small
Or I would get shoved
It took me years
to break free from the bullies
it took me years not to fear feeling again
it took me years
to not
be ashamed of my tears.

Open Up.
What hurts
What burns
That's the place
From which I learn.
When I'm burning
I know that I am learning.

Listen-in II.
I've been hearing so much peace in the silence
If people stopped and listened
There'd be so much less
Violence.

Waking Beauty.
That day Sleeping Beauty stopped waiting for a prince
woke herself
the fuck up.
Just in time to live
Just in time to give
Her self to the world
Just in time for the world
To give itself
Back to her.

Joy is My Job.
Joy is my job
and pleasure
is my priority.

Hunger for Life.
I always ate like I was starving
and I was
but it was not for fucking
food.
I finally turned my hunger
toward life itself
Now I devour pleasure,
Now I gorge on experience
I grow full with joy
and fat with love.

I Dove into Diamonds.
I leapt off that shore of normal
And dove into that sea of diamonds.

I Got Saved
I had a dream, that of a man walking down the concrete
street.
He was Darkness and Captivity, a Patriarchal Society.
He held a group of balloons down by their strings.
I was one of those balloons striving to float up and fly
And somehow my string got snipped and I drifted up to the sky.
My awakening is kind of like that.
I got saved, and I'm just starting to realize why.

You're Not Stuck
We forget
Our emotions are like traffic lights
they don't get stuck on red forever
they are always changing, like the weather.

SACRED SERVICE
Who am I to be a Feminist?
Who am I not to be a Feminist?
Who am I to fight for others' rights?
Who am I not to fight for others' rights?
Who am I to care about global issues?
Who am I not
to care
About global issues?
Everything I do
And say
Affects others and the planet in some way.
Who am I to birth these dreams
that kick & scream inside of me?
The only one.

(I wanted to be the kind of woman who <u>fill in the blank</u>
so I did).

Inner & Outer Cries.
My inner child
and the world
are one.
They say
Please don't close your heart
and please don't close your eyes
please stop
ignoring our cries.

If You Can Make a Difference, Do.
If you can make a difference
(And you can)
Then it's your duty.
If you have a voice
Raise it for those
Who don't have a choice.

Forgetting What She Has.
The problem with the Western Woman
is that she has so much
she forgets
All she has.

High Fives from Nature.
Sometimes
when earth's branches brush my face and thighs
I imagine they are reaching out to give me high fives
They whisper,
"Keep Going, Girl,
Keep Going for this World."

What We Gave.
I don't understand this obsessive need
To hoard and save
When the only thing we leave this world with
Is what we gave.

At Your Door.
Refuse to ignore
The cries of the world
Sooner rather than later
They will be
At your own door.

When the World is Dying
Rock the Boat.
When we're sailing toward death and all the
souls have grown cold
And hearts are drowning
barely staying afloat
Do, do, do
Rock the boat.

While I'm Here.
The world may wake to Love
Long after I am gone
But one thing for me is clear:
I will do my part
While I'm still here.

Use You.
You were given your gift
So you would use it
Not so you would hide it
Or keep it to yourself
Or let it sit dying
On the shelf
You have no more time to doubt
And the world
Can no longer
Go without.
(The. World. Needs. Your. Medicine. Woman.)

Face of Your Heart I.
Can you look softly at the face of your heart?
Can you look so much more softly at you,
and all you've been through?
Can you love even the parts
of you that never came true?
Can you love yourself, from now on,
through everything
that you do?

Isolation.
Oh God, don't you know
it's so lonely in your ego?

Substance Spell.
Mostly I want to do everything naked
with my soul as clear as a bell
But sometimes I drink
just to feel the mist
and fall under its spell.

Feel Better.
Here's some tea
Here's a sweater
Here's a promise
It will all get better.
Here's my goal, that this love
fills every hole
in your soul.

Distractions.
The things she did
to avoid being alone with her loneliness
drove her deeper and deeper into the mess
oh, the lengths you'll go in vain
to avoid your own pain
oh, the substances and the screens
you'll put between
your own cries and the cries of the world.
How many screens
can I place
between myself & my true needs?

[One day my life & the world finally cried
Heyyyy heyyyy heyyyyy
there's no more time
to look away.]

Ship. Wrecked.
She's the girl you root for
who's washed up on the shore
a mess in her tattered wedding dress
destroyed from her final
ship wreck
Her ship went down
And she was sure that
She would drown
But somehow that's how
She finally got found.

Don't Care When They Stare.
She told me not to care
when they stare
she said maybe it isn't fair
but some people are just designed
to always have to dare
and always have to share.

Moth & Flame.

Once upon a time,
there was a little flame,
it's not so important that you know her name,
she just turned and burned in the dark,
and sometimes she'd burn out,
but then, she'd find a spark
and she would rekindle herself for that was all she knew,
was to burn and to die and rise anew,
and that was she all that she had ever done
was burn and yearn without someone
until one day a creature of shadow came
and he began to flit around her flame
so she talked to him throughout the night
but suddenly he began to take her light
and he took and took from her as he hovered
and she begged him to leave as she was smothered,
and he cried, *No we are each others!*
you are my light for a moth needs a flame,
you shall be mine and take my name.
No, she hissed back with her last bit of might
I would rather be alone, in fact even dead
So you really must go now, was what she said
And he yelled, *but I need you, so you must need me,*
the moth and the flame is an old as time story
and a woman needs a man,
don't you understand?
She said, *But I don't need a man, For I am mine,*
(but *maybe* she thought in the back of her mind
maybe there's someone, maybe there's *Just That One,*
for sometimes deep in her dreams, she could feel him come)
But he persisted
Even as she resisted
So as her flame flickered and sighed and threatened to die
the little light thought *perhaps he is right,*
and not I.
maybe this was love
to be smothered by a moth
who swooped in from above
but a little voice inside her fought

no no no - true love, this is not
So she said, *Perhaps you need me*
But I don't need you
You see, I don't do this for you
It's just what I was born to do,
it's how I was made
Like a tree can't help but offer shade
Like the sun I would burn
Even if no one were warmed
I don't shine
For validation
I'm like the moon who glows in the dark air
And the earth who rises with crops to bear.
I would sing even if no one were there
Isn't it enough for you that in the dark, I give light?
Why must you try to claim me with all your might?
And then in the remembrance
of who she was and why she was here
she rose just bravely enough
to cause him fear
And so he finally left her alone
although he said, *you'll want me back, you're too fragile on your own*
and she shook and said *I'd rather feel lonely*
than be with someone who needs to own me,
and so once again she burned her singular way home
and she was sure it would always be that way
but... then... one day
another flame lit up beside her
by some divine grace
and in his fire she could see her own face
what a surprise
to see herself
in another's eyes
I know you she said
he nodded, *this is true*
I promised I'd come back for you
and with that space between them they danced in the air
and when she got weak he would lean over and re-light her with care
and when he grew tired and uninspired,
she'd offer him her own fire
and through lifetimes like that, they burned with their mutual desire
and together their flames only rose higher.
She said *"I didn't realize when I was looking for me*
I'd been looking for you

and when I burned alone in the dark
you would hear my soul like a lark
and how I know that we are true
is that our re-union
is not only for me and not just for you
but in our coming together
we've made the world brighter,
and we've made the world better."

I Love Being a Woman.

I love being a woman.
I love this huge heart of mine,
that breaks at an intimate gust of wind, at the sound of it, moving through a chime.
At my father's sudden vulnerability,
at a comforting smile from a stranger,
with seemingly so much less than me.
For the lost dog on the side of the road, for whom I leap out of my car
to move it out of danger.
This heart, it just breaks and breaks and wakes and wakes.
It's so raw with love for the world, it's so tender and true,
despite all the pain and fear it just keeps walking, shaking, toward
you.
My heart, she's courageous, my heart, she's my hero, my heart, she's my muse.
And only a man with a hero's heart will I choose.
I love being a woman. I love red lipstick that transforms me from simple into siren on a
routine grocery run,
and that I'm way more like the moon than I am the sun.
I love velvet, capes, tight jeans and silk slips,
and I chug the world, I don't take it in sips.
I love being a woman, I love men awakened to their feminine heart, who can bring forth their
soul in their world-changing art.
I love men who are brave and present and masters at decisions,
I love men with big hearts and big brains, big hands and big visions.
I love being a woman. I love that we can stop each other on the street and that's how we meet.
It's *where did you get that bag* and then it's our weddings and miscarriages and divorces,
and then nothing could pull us apart,
not ten thousand horses.
I love being a woman. I love that we love Love so much,
that there is an ocean of emotion inside of us
ready to spill and quake and wake the world at any moment.
And we do, and we will.
Our love is always trembling at the gates, ready to spill.
I love being a woman. I love my beloved's beating heart as my pillow, that's my favorite place
to lay my head,
but when I don't have him, I'll spoon with my dog in my bed.
I love being a woman. I change with the seasons, I grow lusty on fire in summer, I fall in fall,
and I die in winter, only for my heart to sing

again in spring.
Nothing changes like a woman.
I shed skins like the snake,
the stale surface of my old mold breaks
like an earthquake
and up and out the new me rises
and she's always full of so many surprises.
I love being a woman. I love that when my heart breaks it breaks open to hold the whole
world. It's the size of the universe, it's the size of the galaxy,
it's the heart of God, and it's way, way bigger than me.
I cry for Africa and Syria, Libya and Iraq, and the endangered and the voiceless, and I will
keep crying and speaking for the oppressed, abused and the choiceless
because love... love is what this planet is so starved for,
it's the medicine of which we need so much more.
More love and compassion, humanity and humility.
I cry and I cry and my tears taste just like the sea that lives inside of me.
I love being a woman. I am a fool for love but not for fear
and I am learning to take the good risks over the bad, although those still whisper in my ear.
And almost everyday I stand at a cliff,
I stand at the brink and I think,
This could be a phenomenal failure or an epic success, but I will never know unless I leap.
For you'll never know, unless you go
to that place where you're scared
your wings, they only work in the air,
they don't open when you're small, huddled in your lair.
And I am often reminded that the caterpillar, she had to die,
she had to die before she could fly.
I love being a woman. I fail spectacularly at being anyone other than me. And I finally stopped
hiding my true self on the shelf.
I've dusted her off and I've set her free,
I had to just be me, nothing else works, I've tried it all, you see.
I love being a woman. I love that I have ten million dreams and one is to own my own land
and tend to it with my own hands
and save all the rescues
and when I tell this to another woman she says, *"That's my dream too,
and to free all the wild creatures from the circus and the zoo."*
I love being a woman. I love that I fall in love with every man I kiss, and some just that I see,
and some who just live in dreams inside of me.
And that means I can hold a whole lotta love in this church of my heart; at the altar of love is
where I belong, there's a whole gospel choir, singing love's song.

It's a teeming congregation filled to the rafters of every man I've ever loved; you're all lining the pews, you've all been my muse.

Every man who's ever touched me is in there, sharing all that love air.

But there's just one whom I am walking toward.

There's just that one with whom I'll never be bored.

I love being a woman. I'm a woman who finds her story in every song and her song in every story. Dear sister, my story is your story and your story is mine.

If we can lay down our fear and jealousy of each other, we're going to be just fine.

I love being a woman. I honored my Maiden stage for all its bruising brutal teachings but this Mother stage has much deeper reachings. And embraced within the beloved word Mother is that sacred word Other. Serving the other saved me from my self.

The secret to life is service, it's why they call it Secret Service.

You have to share your soul with the world, even if you're nervous.

Now I find myself in the world, not the world in myself.

I was a closed hard bud pushing up through the dark dirt and gasping for breath,

I was a fighter until my Maiden's death.

The bud was my heart that ripped open like a flower,

I'm a lover now, I can receive, I can be devoured.

I love being a woman. I love that my creativity moves like the cycles of the earth,

a seed is planted, germinated, nurtured and birthed.

I empty myself to be filled, just like the moon I grow dark to glow again,

I fall to the floor to rise once more,

I lose my self to re-discover her and become ever more sure

Of who I am and why I'm here,

like the day after a rainstorm, it becomes that much more clear.

I love being a woman with intuition that rips through her like a lightning rod,

like the very voice of God.

I love being a woman. I can feel the earth breathe beneath my bare feet

and have an overwhelming love for every child and creature I meet.

I love being a woman. I have my mother's skin and I have my mother's chin and I have her eyes, her sighs and her thighs.

I love being a woman. The more I give, the more I live

and I sleep and I weep and I laugh and I love and I cry and I don't...

I don't want to die

just to the parts that no longer feel like *I*.

The lines on my face reveal lessons that didn't go to waste

and I'm not growing old, I'm just living more stories to be told

and every day, growing more bold.

I love being a woman. My prayer is *"Dear God, help me help."*

Helping others helps me

and it isn't *I* who will save the world, but *We*.
More than ever I just want to help,
at least a few people feel freer and loved and more okay.
To be a source of comfort and courage in someone's day,
to take them into my velvet lap,
to mine the gold inside of them, to promise, their heart is their map.
I love being a woman. I fell into the dark as a girl, and from winter's womb
was birthed from my tomb
as a woman of the world
sprung into the light of spring.
Now I wake along with everything,
the earth and the trees, the birds and the bees,
and I'm no longer here to please.
I have a voice, I have a choice, and with both I'll do my best,
I'll take the world, like a hungry crying child to my breast
and feed it with my body's love,
I'll be the bearer of peace, I'll ride on the wings of the white dove.
In the depths of my death he broke my heart and he tore apart
my shell.
I walked through three months of fire, I lived through three months of hell.
I learned about ego and isolation, of giving and living, of true femininity and intimacy.
And they weren't… they weren't easy lessons to see.
Oh God, it burned.
Oh God, I learned.
Life, love, it took me and it shook me and it broke me and it woke me and it made me into a
woman.
The bigger the death, the bigger the birth
and as my life unfolds on this earth
I can say that I love, I love being a woman.
The more your heart breaks, the more it can hold
So be brave, my sister, be bold.
And the bigger your heart,
the greater your power
and now, now is the feminine's hour.
The world is starved, it's ravenous for you, and we need all hearts on deck,
if we're going to make it through.
So go ahead, do your part, offer your heart at the world's starving altar.
Go ahead, make the stars shake.
Go ahead, may the world
Wake in your wake.